DOLLY PARTON

The Life of a Legendary American Singer, Actor, and Businesswoman

Newbury Publishing

Thank you for purchasing this Newbury Publishing book.

Get access to FREE ebooks when you sign up for our mailing list. At Newbury Publishing we will only send you emails about free ebooks.

Visit us on our website to sign up at NewburyPub.com.

Copyright © 2022 Newbury Publishing, LLC.

All rights reserved. Except as permitted under the U.S. Copyright Act of 1976, no part of this publication may be reproduced, distributed, or transmitted in any form or by any means, or stored in a database or retrieval system, without the prior written permission of the publisher.

If you would like to use material from the book (other than for review purposes), prior written permission must be obtained by contacting the publisher at permission@newburypub.com. Thank you for your support of the author's rights.

Newbury Publishing, LLC
867 Boylston Street, 5th Floor, PMB 203, Boston, MA 02116

Visit our website at www.newburypub.com

The publisher is not responsible for websites (or their content) that are not owned by the publisher.

Cover and book design by Newbury Publishing, LLC.

The Newbury Publishing name and logo are trademarks of Newbury Publishing, LLC. All rights reserved.

First eBook Edition April 2022

CONTENTS

Title Page
Introduction
Chapter 1: Early Life and Family   1
Chapter 2: Music in the 1960's   5
Chapter 3: Music in the 1970's   9
Chapter 4: Music in the 1980's and 1990's   13
Chapter 5: Music in the 2000's, 2010's, and 2020's   17
Chapter 6: Charity Work   22
Chapter 8: Dollywood   27
Chapter 9: 9 to 5   31
Chapter 10: Personal Life   35
Chapter 11: Discography and Filmography   39
Chapter 12: Awards   46

INTRODUCTION

Dolly Parton is best known for her musical prowess, but there is so much more to her character than people realize. Nowadays, she is the epitome of old Hollywood glamor. She is pretty well known for getting a lot of cosmetic surgery over the years in order to keep up the gaudy, glamorous image we've come to know and love. Even through all this she's still modest. Having received several offers to pose nude for *Playboy Magazine*, she always turned them down; even though she did pose in a bathing suit one time. Even with her modest and humble nature she is still up for a little fun.

What people may not realize is that her early life was anything but glamorous. She wasn't always full of glitz like we see her today. In fact, Parton was raised in a poor family in small town Tennessee. Her childhood story is as country as country gets. However, this tough upbringing would not deter her, and she continued to pursue her musical dreams through ups and downs.

Parton's entertainment career started very young. Though you probably wouldn't call it a career, she was performing at her local church as far back as elementary school. She continued with her education and eventually graduated high school. However, not being one to back down from a challenge, she immediately moved to Nashville after graduation and began pursuing her career in music.

Parton with Porter Wagoner in 1969

Throughout the 1960's and 1970's, Parton fought hard to establish her solo career. It wasn't always easy, but she always persevered. Thanks to influential friends in the industry, such as Porter Wagoner, she was able to finally make it in music. Parton really started to hit commercial success at the beginning of the 1980's. Her music was thriving, and this was also around the same time she had her film-based pop culture breakthrough. However, she struggled a bit in the early 1990's when new artists were quickly overshadowing the veterans in the industry. She pushed through and was able to make a comeback. She continued to face setbacks over the years, but always found a way to fight her way back to the top.

Now, Parton has been able to compose over 5,000 songs throughout her illustrious career. In total, she has recorded and released about 1,100 songs between studio recordings, live tracks, and remixes combined. She has recorded under 11 different record labels, including her own label, Dolly Records. She has been on many national and international tours, and she is still working on releasing new music at the age of 76.

Not only has Parton's career been prolific in terms of the amount of music she has produced, but it has also been incredibly successful in terms of awards and accolades. Regarding her singles and album releases, 21 of them have been certified either Gold or Platinum by the Recording Industry Association of America (RIAA). Twenty-five of her songs have reached number one on the Billboard Hot Country Songs chart. Forty-two of her albums have been in the country top 10. In total, over the past 40 years, Parton has charted 110 singles.

As you can clearly see, Parton's discography is absolutely mind-blowing. Because of how prolific her career has been, she has been able to break a number of records. Some of these include most number one hits from a female country artist and most top 10 country albums. She is also the first artist to produce at least one top 20 hit on Billboard's country chart in six consecutive decades.

Parton's music has evolved between genres over the years. Although she is best known as a country and bluegrass artist, these haven't always been the only genres of music that she has released. It is no secret that Parton has a very unique, and very high, soprano voice. Because of this unique and high sound, record labels initially tried to market her as a pop singer, despite her pleas to record country music. However, they soon learned that, if they would only listen to this musical genius, magic would happen.

Beyond the music, though, Parton is a woman of many talents. She also has an incredible acting career. Since 1956, Parton has appeared on 80 television programs and specials and 14 movies.

One of her movies, *9 to 5*, received very mixed reviews, but still managed to be a big enough hit that it inspired television and Broadway musical spinoffs.

Parton is a savvy businesswoman as well. In addition to owning her own record label, she is also the owner of the Dollywood Company. The Dollywood Company manages a ton of entertainment venues, including the Dollywood theme park, Splash Country Water Park, and multiple dinner theatre venues. She also operates numerous charitable organizations as well. The most famous of these is the Dollywood Foundation, which manages a multitude of projects dedicated to poverty relief and education worldwide.

This has not been Parton's only stint in charity work, though. In fact, she has decades' worth of charity work under her belt. She has donated time and money to various organizations and causes. In addition to the Dollywood Foundation, she is also known for the Imagination Library. This organization sends free books to children around the world on a monthly basis from the time they are born until they get to their first year in school. Education has always been very important for Parton, and she continues to promote it through her philanthropy today.

Parton is not the only famous member of her family and friend circles, either. Several of her siblings have also had successful careers in the music and film industries. Some names you may know include Stella Mae Parton, Randel Huston "Randy" Parton, and Rachel Ann George, who is also known as Rachel Dennison.

Parton is married to Carl Dean. Though the two never had children of their own, the pair have certainly had their hands full helping to raise some of Parton's younger siblings. This has earned them some affectionate nicknames among their nieces and nephews. Additionally, Parton is close friends with the Cyrus family and is the godmother of Miley Cyrus, another American country and pop singer.

CHAPTER 1: EARLY LIFE AND FAMILY

Dolly Parton's life was not always the picture of glamor and beauty that we see today. In fact, her life growing up was the complete opposite. She describes her family in early childhood as "dirt poor". Her parents, Avie Lee Caroline and Robert Lee Parton Sr., worked hard to give their kids the best life they could, though it was not always easy. In fact, her parents had to pay the doctor that delivered her with cornmeal because they were unable to pay in money. Parton pays homage to her family's financial struggles in some of her songs, such as "In the Good Old Days (When Times Were Bad)" and "Coat of Many Colors".

Parton is the fourth of twelve siblings, two of which are twins. Rather than being born with a silver spoon in her mouth, she was born on January 19th, 1946, in a single room log cabin along the bank of the Little Pigeon River. This river is located in Pittman

Center, Tennessee, the town where Parton would spend much of her early childhood. Parton's middle name, Rebecca, comes from her great-great-grandmother on her mother's side of the family, Rebecca Dunn Whitted.

Robert Lee Parton Sr., who also went simply by Lee, worked as a sharecropper in exchange for the home that the family lived in. He would later go on to tend his own small tobacco farm. The tobacco farm had a small income, though. So, to supplement this, Lee also worked various construction jobs to support his family. Parton has credited her father for her business instincts due to this incredible work ethic. Despite the fact that he was illiterate, Parton still states that Lee is one of the most intelligent people she has ever known in regard to business savvy. Lee passed away in 2000.

While Lee was out working, Caroline took care of the family at home. She was a mother of 12 children by the time she was 35 years old. She was typically in poor health, though she worked hard to maintain the home and keep the children entertained. Her family hailed from Wales, and they had immigrated to the Southern Appalachia country over one hundred years prior. The family passed down music through the generations, and Caroline would often sing songs of the Welsh immigrants to the children. She would also entertain them with ancient ballads and Smokey Mountain folklore. Because of this, Parton credits her musical ability to her mother. Caroline passed away in 2003.

Later in Parton's childhood, the family moved from their home in Pittman Center to a farm in Locust Ridge. This is where they would stay for seven or eight years. Many of Parton's childhood memories were made here, and some musical inspiration would also come from this home. Her song "My Tennessee Mountain Home" was inspired by the surrounding woodland. There is also a replica of the Locust Ridge cabin in Dollywood, Parton's theme park.

Parton with a guitar

Parton's maternal grandfather, Jake Owens, served as a Pentecostal preacher in their local church. Because of this, the family spent a significant amount of time at the church. The Church of God in Cleveland Tennessee is also where Parton began her public musical performances. She sang at the church on many occasions, starting at the age of six. At age seven, she learned how to play a homemade guitar. When she was eight years old, her uncle gifted Parton her first real guitar.

As Parton grew up, she would perform on local television and radio shows in the Eastern Tennessee region. She had her first major breakthrough at age 10. It was then that she got to perform on the Cas Walker Show, a variety show that aired on WBIR-TV and WIVK-FM radio in Knoxville, Tennessee.

Parton was signed to a small Louisiana record label, Goldband Records, in her early teen years. By age 13, she recorded the single "Puppy Love". She also got the opportunity as a teenager to perform at the Grand Ole Opry. It was there that she met Johnny Cash. She remembered a piece of advice that he gave her to follow her own instincts when it came to the direction her music career would take.

Despite having already been signed to a record label and appearing in numerous public performances, Parton remained in school. She graduated in 1964 from Sevier County High School in Sevierville, Tennessee. She moved to Nashville the very next day, and that is where her music career really took off.

Stella Mae Parton is the sixth born of the 12 Parton siblings. She is a country music singer and is best known for her 1975 hit "I Want to Hold You in My Dreams Tonight". In addition to her musical talents, Stella Parton has also had quite an illustrious acting career. She starred in numerous Broadway musicals, *Dukes of Hazard*, and many other film and television programs.

Randy Parton is the eighth of the 12 Parton siblings. He is also a country music singer and was the first to record the song "Roll On (Eighteen-Wheeler)", which he recorded two years before the band Alabama did. This would later go on to be Alabama's twelfth number one single. Parton also sang in the soundtrack for the 1984 film, *Rhinestone* and starred in the film as well. Randy Parton passed away from cancer on January 21st, 2021.

Rachel Ann George is the youngest of the Parton siblings. She is also a singer but is best known for her only acting role. In 1982, she starred in the television sitcom rendition of *9 to 5*. George is officially retired, though she does still occasionally sing with her musically inclined siblings.

CHAPTER 2: MUSIC IN THE 1960'S

Parton's music career started in her early childhood, but it only really took off after she graduated from Sevier County High School in 1964. Immediately after graduation, she moved from Locust Ridge to Nashville. This is where many of the great country music stars of all time were made.

However, Parton's road to success was a longer one than you might expect. Despite all of her accomplishments thus far, she was not an immediate smash hit like one might have thought. In fact, it took her years to even be able to record the music that she wanted to record. It would take even longer for her solo career to take off.

Shortly after arriving in Nashville, Parton was signed to Combine Publishing as a songwriter. Her uncle, Bill Owens, acted as a songwriting partner on many of her projects. At this time, she wrote many singles, several of which would later appear on country's top music charts. Some of these would include "Put It Off Until Tomorrow" by Bill Phillips and "Fuel to the Flame" by Skeeter Davis. Hank Williams Jr. and Kitty Wells were among other artists that recorded Parton's music at the time.

Parton was signed to a record label, Monument Records, at age 19. Funnily enough, her label did not initially think that she could make it as a country singer. Due to her very high soprano voice, they tried to pitch her as a bubblegum pop singer. She recorded several singles under this genre, though only one was a minor success. "Happy, Happy Birthday Baby" did manage to hit the charts, but it was not able to crack Billboard's Hot 100 list. Monument Records continued to resist Parton's desire for country music.

Parton's songwriting prowess is what eventually allowed her to follow her country music dreams. "Put It Off Until Tomorrow", on which Parton sang an uncredited harmony, reached number six on the country music charts in 1966. It was then that Monument Records gave in and allowed her to record country music.

Parton's first single was a song called "Dumb Blonde", which reached number 24 on the country music charts in 1967. Her next single, "Something Fishy" went to number 17. These two songs both appeared on Parton's first full-length album, titled "Hello, I'm Dolly", which was released on September 18th, 1967.

"Hello, I'm Dolly" was a bit more successful as a whole album than some of the singles. On the Billboard Top Country Albums chart, it peaked at number 11. It was a much more successful album in the eyes of critics. Billboard described Parton as having a Lolita style "little girl voice" and pointed out several songs on which they felt she did very well. Cashbox said she could "have a big winner in her possession with this striking album". AllMusic gave it a rating of 4.5 stars out of 5.

This is the part of the story where we introduce Porter Wagoner.

He is known as Mr. Grand Ole Opry, which demonstrates the impact he has on country music. Wagoner had a syndicated television series called *The Porter Wagoner Show*. Parton began starring on this show in 1967 after replacing Norma Jean.

Norma Jean Beasler starred on the show from 1961 to 1967. Between 1963 and 1968, she had 13 Billboard Top 40 country singles. Between 1964 and 1973, she recorded 20 albums for RCA Victor. Obviously, Parton had big shoes to fill.

Unfortunately for Parton, she did not quite have the following needed to make this a smooth transition. Wagoner believed in her, but that does not mean that his audience did at the time. In fact, they were pretty ruthless when it came to Parton. They were still upset at Jean's departure, and they were certainly not willing to accept her replacement that easily. Parton explained this tension in her 1994 autobiography. She also mentioned that the audience would even chant Jean's name when Parton came on stage. She persevered, though.

Wagoner had faith in her and decided to see the transition through. He eventually managed to get the audience on his side, and they began to accept Parton. This would be the start of a very successful career for the pair.

Wagoner played a huge role in Parton's next record label signing. He was signed to RCA Victor, the same record label that Norma Jean was signed to, and convinced them to sign Parton as well. The label was hesitant, though, and decided that the first step would be for the pair to record a song together.

The song choice was a remake of "The Last Thing on My Mind" by Tom Paxton. Parton and Wagoner released the duet cover in late 1967. This song reached the top 10 in the country charts in January 1968. Over the next six years, the pair had a pretty much uninterrupted streak of top 10 singles.

1968 was another big year for Parton's solo career in country music. She recorded her first single for RCA Victor as a solo artist, "Just Because I'm a Woman", and it was released in the summer. It became a moderately successful chart hit, topping at number 17. Later in the year, the Country Music Association named Parton and Wagoner the Vocal Group of the Year.

Despite having been one half of the Vocal Group of the Year, Parton's solo records were still being largely ignored by charts and consumers. This includes hits like "In the Good Old Days (When Times Were Bad)", which would eventually become a staple in country music and Parton's record history.

Around this time, Parton had also founded a publishing company, Owe-Par, with Owens. Wagoner showed significant interest and investment in Parton's future as a solo artist. Even when no one else believed in her, he always did. By 1969, he had become co-producer of Owe-Par and owned nearly half of the company.

CHAPTER 3: MUSIC IN THE 1970'S

At the start of the decade, both Wagoner and Parton were continuously frustrated by her lack of solo success despite her obvious talent. Wagoner had the idea that Parton should record a cover of "Mule Skinner Blues" by Jimmie Rodgers. She was not a fan of the idea at first, but eventually relented to it. And it paid off. In February 1971, "Mule Skinner Blues" by Parton went to number three on the charts. Following closely behind was her first single to ever hit number one, "Joshua."

Over the next couple of years, Parton released numerous charting solo singles. These included "Coat of Many Colors", "Touch Your Woman", "My Tennessee Mountain Home", and "Travelin' Man". If you recall, "Coat of Many Colors" and "My Tennessee Mountain Home" were inspired by Parton's childhood growing up in Locust Ridge. She certainly never forgot where she came from, and she has always been very humble about her success.

All of that being said, we would be absolutely remiss if we did not mention Parton's biggest hit of this era, "Jolene". This song still has a great amount of popularity today, which is impressive for a song that is almost 50 years old. This song also represents Parton's first taste of international fame. It was released in late 1973 and reached number one on the country chart in February 1974. It topped out at number 60 on the Billboard Hot 100 chart, and it also hit number seven in the United Kingdom in 1976.

Side A of Parton's hit "Jolene"

Parton performed her final duet with Wagoner in April 1974 after deciding to leave the organization and pursue her solo career. She also stopped appearing on *The Porter Wagoner Show* in mid-1974. However, Parton and Wagoner remained affiliated, and Wagoner helped Parton produce records through 1975. Their final duet album release was on August 18, 1975, with the "Say Forever You'll Be Mine" album.

Backtracking slightly to 1974, Parton wrote her hit song "I Will Always Love You" about her professional split from Porter. Many people do not realize that this was not, in fact, a Whitney Houston original. This song has been covered by many other artists as well, including Linda Ronstadt, LeAnn Rimes, and Kristin Chenoweth.

Interestingly enough, it was this song that *almost* led Parton to striking a deal with Elvis Presley. He wanted to record a version of the song, and Parton was interested in making the deal. However, Presley's manager, Colonel Tom Parker, stepped in and explained that it was a standard procedure for songwriters to sign away half of the publishing rights to any song that Presley recorded. Parton was no longer interested and refused to sign any rights away. This one decision would lead to her making millions of dollars in royalties over the years.

In the mid to late 1970's, Parton began to come around to the idea of being a pop music singer. She has shown a significant influence on pop culture over the years, with the likes of Olivia Newton-John and Emmylou Harris also covering her songs. In 1976, Parton began working closely with Sandy Gallin, an American music producer, who would go on to serve as her personal manager for the next 25 years.

However, Porter Wagoner was not quite out of the picture yet. Together with Gallin and Wagoner, Parton produced her next studio album, entitled "All I Can Do". This album, released on August 16th, 1976, would be one of the last projects of Parton's that Wagoner would have a hand in.

Parton came out with her first self-produced project on February 14th, 1977. This was an album titled "New Harvest…First Gathering", and it was designed to highlight her pop capabilities. This was shown in both the original songs included on the album and the covers, such as "My Girl" by The Temptations and "Higher and Higher" by Jackie Wilson. Sadly, neither the album nor the single "Light of a Clear Blue Morning" made much of an impact in pop culture. On the United States Billboard charts, it reached number 71.

Taking the defeat in stride, Parton then turned to a very well-accomplished pop music producer, Gary Klein, to produce her next album. On October 3rd, 1977, Parton released "Here You Come Again", her 19th solo studio album, under RCA Victor. This album would go on to become her first to sell over one million copies. It became number one on the country chart and reached number 20 on the pop chart. "Here You Come Again", the title track from the album, became Parton's first single to hit the top 10 on a pop chart. It hit number 3. "Two Doors Down" and "It's All Wrong, But It's All Right" each became number one on the country chart and broke into the top 20 on the pop chart. Parton also won a Grammy Award for this album for Best Female Country Vocal Performance.

Throughout the late 1970's, Parton continued to develop her albums with the aim of pop crossover success. And it was a success. Towards the end of the decade, she was moving up both the country and pop charts simultaneously.

To demonstrate how wildly successful Parton was at this time, she had a song in 1979 that was the first single in two years to *not* become number one on the country chart. This was "Sweet Summer Lovin'" off her album "Great Balls of Fire". Now, that is not to say that this song was not at all successful. In fact, it reached number seven on the country chart. However, it only made it to number 77 on Billboard's Hot 100 chart.

But not to worry. Parton would go on to make an amazing pop comeback in 1980 with one of her most iconic songs of all time. It was also in the late 1970's that her film and television career really started to take off as well. She appeared on numerous television specials in the final years of the decade. However, we will touch on this part of her career in a later chapter.

CHAPTER 4: MUSIC IN THE 1980'S AND 1990'S

Parton's commercial success began to grow at the very beginning of the decade. In 1980, she had three consecutive number one hits on the country chart. These were "Starting Over Again", "Old Flames Can't Hold a Candle to You", and "9 to 5". "9 to 5" was written for the comedy movie of the same name. This song reached number one on the country chart, pop chart, and adult contemporary chart in February 1981, which made it a triple number one hit. It was rare for a female country singer to have a number one on both the country and pop chart at the same time, but Parton had accomplished the feat. "9 to 5" received an Academy Award for Best Original Song as well. Parton also released a reunion album with Porter Wagoner this year, and their song "Making Plans" was a top 10 chart hit.

In 1982, Parton re-recorded "I Will Always Love You" for that year's film, *The Best Little Whorehouse in Texas*. This re-recording was not Parton's most successful venture, but it did crack the top 50. She also recorded the classic, "Islands in the Stream", with Kenny Rogers. "Islands in the Stream" spent two weeks in the number one spot in 1983.

Between 1981 and 1985, Parton had 12 top 10 hits. Half of these reached number one. The mid-1980's saw strong record sales for Parton. This included both country and crossover hits. Unfortunately, RCA Victor did not seem to be very impressed with Parton's success. In 1986, Parton's contract with RCA Victor expired, and the company chose not to renew it. This led to Parton signing with Columbia Records in 1987.

The late 1980's saw Parton return to her country and bluegrass roots. In 1987, she released "Trio", a collaborative project with Emmylou Harris and Linda Ronstadt that completely revitalized her career. This album was number one on the country chart for five weeks, and it also made an appearance on Billboard's Top 200 Albums chart."

Unfortunately, the revival was short lived. Around this time, contemporary country music began taking over the charts, and newer artists were quickly pushing out the veterans. Parton had several successful hits in the early 1990's, though. Her greatest commercial success came from Whitney Houston recording her version of "I Will Always Love You" for the film, *The Bodyguard*.

Over the next few years, Parton's career had some ups and downs. She continued to record songs for movies, such as *Straight Talk* in 1992. Sadly, this soundtrack album was not nearly as successful as "I Will Always Love You".

However, Parton bounced back in 1993 with her album "Slow Dancing with the Moon". Also in 1993, Parton recorded "The Day

I Fell in Love" with James Ingram for the film, *Beethoven's 2nd*. The songwriters, Ingram, Carole Bayer Sager and Clif Magness, were nominated for the Academy Award for Best Original Song. Parton and Ingram performed "The Day I Fell in Love" at the Academy Awards telecast. Later in 1993, Parton released a collaboration album with Tammy Wynette and Loretta Lynn, entitled "Honky Tonk Angels". This album was very successful, and the Recording Industry Association of America certified it Gold on January 5th, 1994.

Later in 1994, Parton contributed her talent toward fighting the AIDS and HIV epidemic. She contributed her song, "You Gotta Be My Baby", to the "Red Hot + Country" album produced by the Red Hot Organization. The Red Hot Organization is a nonprofit dedicated to raising awareness and donations for AIDS and HIV relief worldwide. They accomplish this through compilation albums, television programs, and various other media events.

A couple weeks later, P arton decided to do something a little different. She released a live acoustic album, called "Heartstrings: Live from Home", on September 27th, 1994. This album was recorded at a concert in Dollywood. It featured a number of Parton's original songs as well as a slew of traditional folk songs. One of the songs, "To Daddy", had been previously written by Parton, but never recorded by her. An earlier version was released by Emmylou Harris in 1978. However, this was the first time that Parton had recorded the song herself. Another classic that's important to note here is "PMS Blues". This campy comedy song is exactly what you think it is from the title. This classic quickly became a concert favorite. It also got a significant amount of airplay.

Parton remained at a steady pace with her music releases in the mid to late 1990's. She released a cover album in 1996. This album, entitled "Treasures", featured a ton of diverse songs from various 1960's and 1970's artists, such as Pete Seeger, Mac Davis, Cat Stevens, Neil Young, and Kris Kristofferson. Interestingly enough, one of these covers, "Peace Train" by Cat Stevens, was later remixed as a dance song. The dance remix made it onto Billboard's dance singles chart.

Parton branched out again in 1998, releasing a country-rock again called "Hungry Again". This album did not perform well on the charts. However, two of the music videos, "(Why Don't More Women Sing) Honky Tonk Songs" and "Salt in my Tears", received significant airplay on CMT. Just a few months later, Decca Records, Parton's record label at the time, closed its doors and Parton was left without a label. This wouldn't last, though.

Parton went back to a more contemporary style in the following year. She released "Trio II", a collaboration album with Emmylou Harris and Linda Ronstadt. Parton also achieved one of her biggest career successes thus far this year. She was inducted into the Country Music Hall of Fame. This museum is one of the world's largest, and it serves as a research center for the interpretation and preservation of American vernacular music. To date, there have been 146 total inductees into the Country Music Hall of Fame. Only 14 of them have been solo female performers. Parton was the eighth.

In late 1999, Parton returned to her bluegrass roots with her album, "The Grass Is Blue", which was her first bluegrass album. This won a Grammy Award for Best Bluegrass Album. The album was her first release on the independent record label, Sugar Hill Records, and her own label, Blue Eye Records.

CHAPTER 5: MUSIC IN THE 2000'S, 2010'S, AND 2020'S

Parton continued on her bluegrass route for the next several years. In 2001, she released "Little Sparrow". The cover of "Shine" by Collective Soul won a Grammy Award for the Best Female Country Vocal Performance. Her next bluegrass album, "Halos & Horns" came out in 2002. She took a risk for this one and recorded a bluegrass version of Led Zeppelin's "Stairway to Heaven".

In 2005, Parton released "Those Were the Days", an album which featured a number of cover songs, such as "Imagine", "Where Do The Children Play?", "Crimson and Clover", and "Where Have All the Flowers Gone?". These were folk rock era songs from the late 1960's and early 1970's.

Parton had faced a number of ups and downs in her career up to this point. However, 2005 had one of her most controversial events to that date. She recorded her original song, "Travelin' Thru", which was written specifically for the film, *Transamerica*. Despite the early 2000's being a somewhat progressive time, it was not nearly as progressive as our society is today. The film was about transgender awareness and acceptance, and not all of Parton's viewers were ready to embrace this part of society. In fact, a good portion of people became quite enraged with the fact that Parton worked on this project. She received several death threats, though obviously nothing ever came of them.

These struggles were short lived, though. In October 2005, Parton teamed up with Brad Paisley to record a harmony version of "When I Get Where I'm Going". The song debuted at number 50 on the Billboard chart. However, it peaked at number one on Billboard's Hot Country Songs chart and number 39 on Billboard's Hot 100. It won Video of the Year and Vocal Event of the Year through the Academy of Country Music Awards.

Parton released a huge musical project on October 27th, 2009. This was a four-CD box set that included 99 songs and covered a majority of Parton's career. Around this time, she also released a second live album and DVD, which was filmed at her 2008 London concert. The concert was sold out.

In 2011, Parton showed the world that she had not lost anything in the way of talent or fans when she embarked on the Better Day World Tour. The tour included shows in both the United States and Europe.

Three years later, she embarked on yet another world tour, the Blue Smoke World Tour, to promote her 42nd studio album. Interestingly, the United States was not the first country to be graced with the "Blue Smoke" album. In a very wise business decision, Parton released this album in New Zealand and Australia on January 31st, 2014, in order to increase the hype for the upcoming

February concerts. The album reached the top 10 in both New Zealand and Australia.

When it was released in the United States on May 13th, 2014, it debuted on the Billboard 200 chart at number six. This meant that "Blue Smoke" was Parton's first top 10 album and her highest charting solo album in her entire career. It reached number two on the United States country chart.

"Blue Smoke" was released on June 9th, 2014, in Europe and it reached number two on the United Kingdom's album chart. Parton performed at the Glastonbury Festival for the first time on June 29th, 2014, to a group of approximately 180,000 fans.

On March 6th, 2016, Parton announced another tour to promote her next album, "Pure & Simple". This tour was highly significant as it was Parton's largest tour in the United States in over 25 years. It has 64 tour dates total, destined for various locations in the United States and Canada. She also made a point to visit highly requested venues that had been missed on previous tours.

Parton continued to branch out with her music at this point in her career. In 2016, she did a version of "Jolene" with the acapella group, Pentatonix. She would later perform this version on the television series, *The Voice*, alongside Pentatonix and Miley Cyrus.

Parton was also invited to perform on "Forever Country", a song mashup, in 2016. This was quite the honor as only 30 artists in total performed on the track. The song was designed to celebrate 50 years of the CMA Awards. At the CMA Awards that year, Parton was awarded the Willie Nelson Lifetime Achievement Award. Preceding the award, Parton received a tribute from Jennifer Nettles, Reba McIntyre, Pentatonix, Carrie Underwood, Martina McBride, and Kacey Musgraves.

Parton with Willie Nelson

Parton stepped into the pop genre once again in 2017 when she appeared on a duet with Kesha of "Old Flames Can't Hold a Candle to You". A fun fact about this song is that it had been cowritten by Kesha's mother, Pebe Sebert. It was a big hit for Parton after it appeared on her 1980 album, "Dolly, Dolly, Dolly". Parton also cowrote and provided some vocals on "Rainbowland" by Miley Cyrus, Parton's goddaughter.

In 2020, Parton's music hit home for a lot of people when she released her single, "When Life is Good Again". She released this as a response to the Covid-19 pandemic in hopes of keeping spirits up. The music video premiered on May 28th, 2020, on *Time 100*. Parton continued the good news in August of 2020 when she announced that she would be putting out her first holiday album in over 30 years. The album is titled, "A Holly Dolly Christmas". On December 6th, 2020, a Christmas special aired on CBS called *A Holly Dolly Christmas*. Parton performed several of her new holiday songs on this Christmas special.

Parton recently released her 48th studio album, which is titled

"Run, Rose, Run". The album was released on March 4th, 2022. The album will be released alongside a book of the same name, on which Parton worked with James Patterson, an American author. So far, two singles from the album have been released. They are "Big Dreams and Faded Jeans" and "Blue Bonnet Breeze". In total, the album will have 12 original songs.

CHAPTER 6: CHARITY WORK

Of course, nearly everyone knows Parton best for her musical ability. However, what you may not realize is the sheer scale of her charity work over the years. She has invested a ton of money and time into various charities over her career. Let's look at a quick overview.

One of Parton's earliest, and perhaps most famous philanthropic endeavors is the Dollywood Foundation. Established in 1988, the foundation was named after Parton's theme park, which we will discuss in the next chapter. The original purpose of the Dollywood Foundation was to support educational achievement in the Sevier County, Tennessee region. The foundation would eventually morph into the Imagination Library in 1995.

The Imagination Library provides free books to children across the world every year from birth until their first year in school. This foundation is inspired by Parton's father, who was illiterate. When it was first established, it was a United States only program. Participants receive one book every month. It went international in 2006 by expanding to Canada and the United Kingdom. It expanded to Australia in 2013.

In the late 1980's, Parton established the Buddy Program. This program was established shortly after the Dollywood Foundation. It was designed as another effort to help children and teenagers in the Sevier County region. The program established a buddy system between 7th and 8th grade students in the area. If both buddies in the pair successfully graduated high school, then each person in the pair would receive $500 cash. According to research conducted by the organization, Parton's gift helped the high school dropout rate decrease from 35% to 6%.

Around the same time, Parton bestowed another gift to older students in Sevier County. In 1989, Parton gifted $500 to every high school student that wished to attend Hiwassee College in an effort to improve graduation rates and college attendance.

In 1991, Parton turned her attention to our feathered friends. She established the Eagle Mountain Sanctuary in Dollywood. The 30,000 square feet of aviary houses are managed by the American Eagle Foundation. These house the world's largest collection of non-releasable bald eagles. These eagles are on display for park visitors for several months every year, and they also participate in the Wings of America Birds of Prey show.

Returning to educational projects, Parton established the Dolly Parton Scholarship in 2000. This scholarship is awarded to five Sevier County students each year. The winner of the scholarship receives $15,000 to pursue educational goals. The Dollywood Foundation notes that the scholarship is designed for students who "have a dream they wish to pursue and who can successfully communicate their plan and commitment to realize their dreams."

In 2002, the Dollywood Foundation established the Chasing Rainbows Award. The National Network of State Teachers of the Year works in conjunction with this award. It is awarded to teachers who have overcome obstacles in their lives and dedicate themselves to making a difference in children's lives. The winner of this award gets to spend one week in Dollywood as Parton's honored guest.

In 2007, Parton turned her attention to the medical needs of Sevier County. Performing at a benefit concert in May 2007, Parton raised $500,000 for the LeConte Medical Center. In addition, Parton's Dixie Stampede dinner theater and Dollywood also pledged $250,000 each, totaling $1 million for the new hospital. In 2010, the hospital named the women's health ward after Parton.

2016 was a huge year for Parton's charity work. She established the My People Fund, which was in response to the wildfires in the Great Smokey Mountains. This movement raised $1,000 per month for six months. Parton also hosted two telethons to raise money for victims of the fires. In addition, Parton awarded scholarships to graduating high school seniors who had lost their homes in the fires. Also in 2016, Parton awarded a $30,000 Special Merit Scholarship to celebrate the Imagination Library reaching the milestone of one million books per month. Parton also came out in support of transgender rights later that year.

Parton with U.S. Senators Bob Corker, Richard Burr, Lamar Alexander, and Congressman John Duncan, with others, the Great Smoky Mountains National Park

Going back to medical charities, Parton donated $1 million to the Monroe Carell Jr. Children's Hospital in 2017. She made the donation in honor of her niece, who was treated for leukemia at that very hospital.

2018 was another big year for Parton. The Imagination Library celebrated its milestone of giving out 100 million books. Currently, the program has given out over 1.3 million books to children worldwide. In addition to the money she donated to the Monroe Carell Jr. Children's Hospital, Parton also helped establish the Hannah Dennison Butterfly Garden, named after her niece that was treated at the hospital.

In addition to the music she released to help raise spirits during the Covid-19 pandemic, Parton also donated money. She gave $1 million to the Vanderbilt University Medical Center to fund vaccine research.

Parton still has not stopped her giving ways. Even two years into an international crisis, she continues to take care of those that loyally serve her theme park. In February 2022, Parton announced that Dollywood would provide full tuition coverage, including books and some other expenses, for employees.

These are just a few of the highlights of Parton's career. She has also donated to and participated in a number of other causes, such as the American Red Cross and PETA. Parton has received numerous awards for her charitable efforts as well. Some of these include the Association of American Publishers Honors Award, Good Housekeeping Seal of Approval, American Association of School Administrators Galaxy Award, National State Teachers of the Year Chasing Rainbows Award, and Parents as Teachers National Center Child and Family Advocacy Award. Interestingly, Parton's Good Housekeeping Seal of Approval was the first time that it had been awarded to an individual person.

On May 8th, 2009, Parton gave the commencement speech at the University of Tennessee Knoxville's College of Arts and Sciences. During the ceremony, she was awarded an honorary Doctor of Humane Letters degree. This was only the second time an honorary degree had been bestowed by the university.

CHAPTER 8: DOLLYWOOD

Even if you did not know much about Dolly Parton before reading this book, you are sure to have heard of Dollywood. This world-famous theme park has become a right of passage for adrenaline junkies and country music enthusiasts. It has a long history spanning decades, multiple owners, and billions of dollars in upgrades.

The theme park now known as Dollywood has been around for six decades, but it has not always been known as Dollywood. The park opened in 1961 and was owned by the Robbins brothers of Blowing Rock, North Carolina. The original name was Rebel Railroad. The park was modeled after the Robbins brothers' first theme park, Tweetsie Railroad in Blowing Rock, which was very successful. This new park featured a general store, saloon, blacksmith shop, and steam train. Themed after the Civil War's centennial anniversary, the train ride featured staged attacks from Native

Americans, train robbers, and Union soldiers. Actors playing Confederate soldiers would protect riders from the attacks.

The first major update to the park came in 1971. Art Modell, then owner of the Cleveland Browns, bought the park and renamed it Goldrush Junction. Modell kept the train ride and added a log flume ride, outdoor theater, and Robert F. Thomas Church.

The second major update to the park occurred in 1976. Jack and Pete Herschend purchased Goldrush Junction and renamed it Goldrush for its 1976 season. They renamed it again in 1977 to Silver Dollar City Tennessee. This was now a sister park to the Silver Dollar City theme park in Branson, Missouri. The Herschends spent approximately $1 million upgrading the park over the years. In 1977, they added two steam locomotives, numbers 70 and 71 from the White Pass & Yukon Route Railroad.

Parton grew up in the area and took a liking to Silver Dollar City. In 1986, she bought an interest in the park. Along with this purchase came a deal for the park to be named Dollywood for the 1986 season. Parton stated that she became involved with the park because she wanted to come back to the area if she ever made it big in order to something great for her part of the country and bring various jobs to the area. Also in 1986, several new attractions were added. These included several new rides and "Rags to Riches: The Dolly Parton Story", a museum dedicated to the retelling of Parton's life story. In the first season as Dollywood, park attendance doubled, and the park received more than one million guests that year. More rides, including several children's rides, were added in 1987, 1988, and 1989. In 1988, the park also got the Celebrity Theater.

Over the next several decades, many more rides and park areas would cycle through the park. In 2001, Dollywood's Splash Country, a 25-acre water park, opened next to the Dollywood parking lot. In 2002, a new museum, Chasing Rainbows, opened in the park. This museum currently features 29 exhibits. There is also a former tour bus, known as Dolly's Home-On-Wheels, located in the front of the museum. Guests are able to enter the bus and take pictures.

2009 saw a first for the nation thanks to Dollywood. SkyZip, an entertainment company owned by Skyline Eco-Adventures of Hawaii, expanded to Dollywood. This culminated in the installation of the first multiple line zipline tour within a theme park.

Dollywood has won a number of awards. In 2017 and 2018, Amusement Today has presented the park with several awards for Friendliest Park, Best Food, Best Show, and Best Christmas Event. In 2018, the park was ranked number six Best Amusement Park on USA Today's 10 Best Readers' Choice Awards. For the Best Amusement Park Hotel category, Dollywood's DreamMore Resort and Spa ranked number one. For the Best Amusement Park Restaurant, Dollywood's Aunt Granny's Restaurant ranked number one. For the Best Amusement Park Entertainment category, Dollywood's Dreamland Drive-In ranked number three. For the Best Outdoor Water Park category, Dollywood's Splash Country ranked number six. In 2019, Dollywood won more Golden Ticket Awards for Best Guest Experience, Best Kids' Area, and Best Christmas Event of 2018. That year, Lightning Rod, a roller coaster at the park, won Wooden Coaster of the Decade. In 2021, Smokey Mountain Christmas won the Golden Ticket Award for Best Christmas Event. This was the 13th year in a row that this show won the Golden Ticket Award for Best Christmas Event.

In its current state, Dollywood has 11 themed areas. These are Adventures in Imagination, Country Fair, Craftsman's Valley, Owens Farm, Jukebox Junction, Rivertown Junction, Showstreet, Timber Canyon, The Village, Wilderness Pass, and Wildwood Grove. Throughout these areas, there are over 50 rides, nine theaters, nine general shows, and eight festival of nations shows. It is also the host of several of the South's biggest yearly festivals. There are numerous Christmas shows that play each year as well. Dollywood also features 10 master craftsmen and 14 characters. The 150-acre park employs more than 4,000 employees.

But Parton is not stopping there. Over the past few years, she has announced numerous plans for expansion of the park and services offered. In October 2019, Dollywood filed plans to add a new resort which will be adjacent to Splash Country and DreamMore Resort. Planned features for this new resort include a 310-room hotel, 325-seat restaurant, and conference spaces. The resort is planned to create over 100 new jobs. Additional plans, totaling approximately $500 million, were announced in June 2021. The name was revealed to be HeartSong Lodge & Resort. This is scheduled to open in 2023, though an exact launch date has not yet been determined. This new resort is planned to have three additional resorts, campgrounds, and a new attraction that is set to break a theme park record. An announcement was made on November 3rd, 2021, that the Pigeon Forge Planning Commission approved the expansion.

Parton has stated that she would eventually like to open multiple Dollywood locations throughout the country. It is also a possibility that it could expand internationally someday as well.

CHAPTER 9: 9 TO 5

The movie *9 to 5* was Parton's biggest pop culture breakthrough. This is an American comedy movie directed by Colin Higgins. In the film, Parton plays Doralee Rhodes, the victim of sexual harassment by her less than savory boss, Frank Hart. Hart goes on to spread a rumor that the two are having an affair, which causes other staff members to shun Rhodes. The movie then follows Rhodes and two coworkers, Judy Bernly and Violet Newstead, as they exact their revenge on their evil boss.

The movie received mixed reviews by critics and audiences. However, the music was a huge hit. The title song, "9 to 5", won Grammy Awards for Best Country Vocal Performance, Female and Best Country Song. It was also nominated for Song of the Year. It won a People's Choice Award for Favorite Motion Picture Song as well. The movie, itself, was nominated for a Grammy Award for Best Album of Original Score Written for a Motion Picture or Television Special. Interestingly enough, the soundtrack was a bigger hit in Australia than the United States. It peaked at number 33 in Australia and number 77 in the United States and tt was certified platinum in Australia.

The film also inspired a number of spin-offs, including a television series and a Broadway musical. The television series, also titled *9 to 5* lasted for five seasons and aired on ABC. In total, there were 85 episodes. The television series, sadly, saw a lot of turnover. Rachel Dennison is the only actress that appeared on the show throughout its entire run. The theme song was taken from the film, though the first season featured Phoebe Snow's vocals rather than Parton's. From season two onward, Parton's vocals were featured in the theme song. There were some noticeable plot differences between the film and the television series, such as family members, romantic relationships, and character personalities and backgrounds.

In 2005, rumors began circulating about a *9 to 5* movie sequel. In 2018, Parton announced officially that a sequel was in the works. However, she later stated on October 30th, 2019, that the sequel had been dropped. There have been no further talks of a sequel since then.

Parton appeared on *Larry King Live* on September 30th, 2005, where she revealed that she was working on music for a musical theater adaptation of *9 to 5*. An initial reading of the musical took place on January 19th, 2007. During the week of June 20th, 2007, a team of writers workshopped a revised draft. There was an industry presentation in New York on June 28th, 2007.

The *9 to 5* musical premiered in Los Angeles on September 20th, 2008. The show ran through October 19th, 2008. It won two Los Angeles Drama Critics Circle Awards, which were for the Musical Score (written by Parton) and for the Choreography.

But all was not perfectly fine in the theater world of *9 to 5*. The estate of Colin Higgins filed a lawsuit against Higgins' former attorney. The basis of the lawsuit was that this attorney failed to secure stage rights of the musical for Higgins.

This would not hold the project back, though. *9 to 5* had its official Broadway opening at the Marquis Theatre on April 30th, 2009. Production closed on September 6th, 2009. In total, there were 24 previews and 148 regular performances of the musical.

The show didn't stop there either. There was a national tour the following year, which began on September 21st, 2010, at the Tennessee Performing Arts Center in Nashville. The tour lasted for 10 months and concluded at the Bass Performance Hall in Forth Worth, Texas on July 31st, 2011. About a year and a half later, on October 12th, 2012, the United Kingdom tour kicked off at the Manchester Opera House. This tour finished at the Manchester Opera House on August 24th, 2013.

Parton at the Grand Ole Opry in Nashville

It would be several years before any other majorly significant performances occurred. However, it started up again on February

17th, 2019, at the Savoy Theatre in the West End. The show received two extensions and was supposed to run until May of 2020. Sadly, production had to shut down early due to the Covid-19 pandemic. The show was also supposed to have an Australia run in 2020, but this has been indefinitely postponed due to Covid-19. Luckily, Covid did not stop the second national United Kingdom tour, which launched on August 31st, 2021, at the Mayflower Theatre Southampton. There has also been a number of regional performances throughout the United States.

There are two recordings of the musical. The first is the recording of the original Broadway cast. This was recorded on May 3rd and 4th, 2009, at New York's Legacy Recording Studios. It was made available on July 14th, 2009, through Parton's official website and all other digital formats. This cast recording was nominated for a Grammy Award for Best Musical Show Album. The second recording is that of the West End cast, which was released on February 7th, 2020. This was recorded live at the Savoy Theatre.

Like the movie, the musical received mixed reviews from critics and audiences. Most of the reviews indicated that, while it was a decent show, it lacked substance and that extra piece of magic that would take it to a top tier show. However, other reviews, such as The Guardian, praised the show and called it a triumph for Parton.

Regardless of the initial mixed reviews, the show did manage to win several awards and numerous nominations. In addition to the Los Angeles Drama Critics Circle Awards, the Los Angeles show was nominated for six LA Ovation Awards. The Broadway production was, unsurprisingly, much more successful. Allison Janney, who played Violet Newstead, won a Drama Desk Award for Outstanding Actress in a Musical. It was nominated for 12 other Drama Desk Awards. It was also nominated for two Drama League Awards, a Grammy Award, three Outer Critics Circle Awards, and four Tony Awards. In total, 15 cast and production members received award nominations.

CHAPTER 10: PERSONAL LIFE

Parton is married to Carl Dean, a down to earth asphalt contractor that never wanted to be a part of the big time. Because he is so private, not many fans know a whole lot about him. But here's what we do know.

Parton and Dean met at a laundromat in 1964 in Nashville. Parton stated that they met the day that she moved to Nashville to pursue her musical career. Dean described the encounter as love at first sight. He has been quoted as saying "My first thought was 'I'm gonna marry that girl.' My second thought was, 'Lord she's good lookin.'"

Though Parton had left behind two boyfriends and was certainly not on the lookout for a new one, she couldn't help but feel an instant connection to Dean as well. She invited him to visit her at her aunt and uncle's house, where she was staying at the time. He visited her there every day for a week. On their first actual date, he took her to meet his parents.

Dean later joined the military, though the two stayed in touch during his military service. After his two-year enlistment ended, Dean popped the question. The happy occasion nearly turned to disaster, though, since Parton's record label was heavily opposed to her getting married. They feared that it would negatively impact her image and career, and they tried to convince her not to go through with it. However, Parton was deeply in love and very hardheaded, so she went through with the marriage. However, they did decide to keep the wedding news on the down low. The two married at a small ceremony in Georgia on May 30th, 1966. In honor of their 50th wedding anniversary, the couple renewed their vows in May 2016.

Dean was always very supportive of Parton's musical career. The day after their wedding, she had to get up early for a radio appearance. The couple's honeymoon was also delayed due to musical commitments.

Funnily enough, Dean is really not a fan of Parton's music since he is more into hard rock. He has inspired several of her biggest hits, though. Some of these include "From Here to the Moon and Back", "Forever Love", "Say Forever You'll Be Mine", and "Tomorrow is Forever". The song "Just Because I'm a Woman" is inspired by Dean's disappointment in finding out that Parton had slept with other men before she got together with him. The song "Jolene" is inspired partially by a bank teller who flirted with Dean one day. Dean, although a very private person, also appears on the album cover for "My Blue Ridge Mountain Boy".

Despite being in a happy relationship, Parton has not always been safe from rumors. In fact, she was accused at one point of being married to cover up a homosexual relationship with her friend, Judy Ogle. She told Vanity Fair in 1991, "She's not my lover; she's never been my lover…If we were lovers, I would not be ashamed of it, I'd just say there's a great love between us. So there." After her role in *The Best Little Whorehouse in Texas*, Parton was rumored to have an affair with her costar, Burt Reynolds. Dean was never bothered by any of these rumors, and the two are very confident in their relationship.

The pair describe themselves as complete opposites. Dean typically doesn't travel with her, though the two say that distance and separation over the years have only strengthened their relationship. That said, Dean has visited with Parton on tour. On one occasion, he even joined her backup singers and became a part of the performance.

Although he is not heavily involved in her musical career, Parton and Dean have a very strong relationship. She has also noted that he has a romantic and creative side to him. She explained that, on several occasions, he wrote poems for her. He also gives her other spontaneous surprises as well.

The couple does not have children of their own. However, Parton is the godmother of singer, Miley Cyrus. You may wonder how Cyrus got so lucky. Well, she has her famous father, Billy Ray Cyrus, to thank for it. Billy Ray Cyrus frequently toured with Parton back in the day. Parton describes a young Miley as "having a light about her" and states that she always knew there was something special about Cyrus. Parton has also appeared on *Hannah Montana* as Cyrus' fairy godmother.

In addition, the couple also helped to raise some of Parton's younger siblings. Some of their nieces and nephews even refer to them as "Uncle Peepaw" and "Aunt Granny". If that sounds familiar, it's because it was the inspiration for one of the Dollywood restaurants.

It wasn't only the couple's choice to not have children, though. Sadly, Parton suffered from endometriosis. This medical condition causes the tissues that typically grow inside the uterus to grow outside of the uterus. As this can be seriously threatening to a woman's health, Parton eventually had to undergo a hysterectomy, a procedure in which the uterus is removed. As such, she was rendered unable to get pregnant. Even without the hysterectomy, though, it is possible that Parton still would've been unable to have children. Some symptoms of this condition include pain, heavy menstrual cycles, and infertility. The infertility occurs in about half of the population affected by this condition. The fatality rate from this condition is very low, though it can cause quite a serious amount of discomfort throughout a woman's life. Ogle supported Parton a lot throughout the time she was dealing with these medical issues.

Parton was very outspoken during the Covid-19 pandemic. She donated $1 million to the Vanderbilt University Medical Center for vaccine research. This donation funded critical early-stage development of the Moderna vaccine. Parton was vaccinated, herself, in March of 2021 and took to social media to encourage others to do the same. She even gave a performance celebrating the vaccine set to the tune of "Jolene".

CHAPTER 11: DISCOGRAPHY AND FILMOGRAPHY

Parton recorded the following albums with Porter Wagoner:
- Just Between You and Me (1968)
- Just the Two of Us (1968)
- Always, Always (1969)
- Porter Wayne and Dolly Rebecca (1970)
- Once More (1970)
- Two of a Kind (1971)
- The Right Combination (Insert date)
- Burning the Midnight Oil (1972)
- Together Always (1972)
- We Found It (1973)
- Love and Music (1973)

- Porter 'n' Dolly (1974)
- Say Forever You'll Be Mine (1975)
- Porter & Dolly (1980)
- Here Comes the Freedom Train (non-album single) (1973)
- Is Forever Longer than Always (non-album single) (1976)

Parton recorded the following albums as a solo artist:
- Hello, I'm Dolly (1967)
- Just Because I'm a Woman (1968)
- In the Good Old Days (When Times Were Bad) (1969)
- My Blue Ridge Mountain Boy (1969)
- The Fairest of Them All (1970)
- The Golden Streets of Glory (1971)
- Joshua (1971)
- Coat of Many Colors (1971)
- Touch Your Woman (1972)
- My Favorite Songwriter, Porter Wagoner (1972)
- My Tennessee Mountain Home (1973)
- Bubbling Over (1973)
- Jolene (1974)
- Love Is Like a Butterfly (1974)
- The Bargain Store (1975)
- Dolly (1975)
- All I Can Do (1976)
- New Harvest…First Gathering (1977)
- Here You Come Again (1977)
- Heartbreaker (1978)
- Great Balls of Fire (1979)
- Dolly, Dolly, Dolly (1980)
- 9 to 5 and Odd Jobs (1980)
- Heartbreak Express (1982)
- Burlap & Satin (1983)
- The Great Pretender (1984)
- Real Love (1985)

- Rainbow (1987)
- White Limozeen (1989)
- Home for Christmas (1990)
- Eagle When She Flies (1991)
- Slow Dancing with the Moon (1993)
- Something Special (1995)
- Treasures (1996)
- Hungry Again (1998)
- Precious Memories (1999)
- The Grass Is Blue (1999)
- Little Sparrow (2001)
- Halos & Horns (2002)
- For God and Country (2003)
- Those Were the Days (2005)
- Backwoods Barbie (2008)
- Better Day (2011)
- Blue Smoke (2014)
- Pure & Simple (2016)
- I Believe in You (2017)
- A Holly Dolly Christmas (2020)
- Run, Rose, Run (2022)

Parton recorded the following albums in partnership with other artists:

- Once Upon a Christmas (1984): with Kenny Rogers
- Trio (1987): with Emmylou Harris and Linda Ronstadt
- Honky Tonk Angels (1993): with Loretta Lynn and Tammy Wynette
- Trio II (1999): with Emmylou Harris and Linda Ronstadt

Parton recorded the following as non-album singles:

- Puppy Love (1959)
- So Little I Wanted, So Little I Got (1962)
- It's Sure Gonna Hurt (1962)
- What Do You Think About Lovin' (1964)
- Happy, Happy Birthday Baby (1965)

- Busy Signal (1966)
- Don't Drop Out (1966)
- Why, Why, Why (1967)
- I'm Not Worth the Tears (1968)
- Comin' for to Carry Me Home (1971)
- Change It (2009)
- Comin' Home for Christmas (2009)
- God Only Knows (2019)

Parton has also recorded a number of singles for various movies and albums by other artists. She has an extensive film and television resumé in addition to her impressive music career. The following is a list of television appearances she made as herself. This does not include award shows. For a list of awards, please see the next chapter.

- Cas Walker Farm and Home Hour (1956-1964)
- The Early Morning Show (1964)
- The Ralph Emery Early Morning Show (1967)
- Music City USA (1967)
- The Wilburn Brothers Show (1967, 1973)
- The Porter Wagoner Show (1967-1974)
- An Old-Time Country Christmas (1969)
- Hee Haw (1970, 1972, 1975)
- The Nashville Sound (1970)
- The Mike Douglas Show (1970, 1974, 1977)
- The David Frost Show (1971)
- That Good Ole Nashville Music (1971)
- The Rowan and Martin Special (1973)
- Burt Reynold's Late Show (1973)
- Dinah's Place (1974)
- In Concert (1975)
- Sing Country 1975 (1975)
- The Ronnie Prophet Show (1975)
- Candid Camera (1975)
- Grand Ole Opry 50th Anniversary (1975)

- Dinah! (1976)
- Dolly! (1976-1977)
- Festival of Entertainment (1976)
- Sing Country 1976 (1976)
- The Mac Davis Show (1976)
- The Hollywood Squares (1976, 1978)
- Captain Kangaroo (1977)
- Mac Davis: Sounds Like Home (1977)
- Musikladen (1977)
- Cher... Special (1978)
- 50 Years of Country Music (1978)
- Dolly & Carol in Nashville (1979): also played Trudy
- The Seventies: An Explosion of Country Music (1979)
- A Christmas Special... With Love, Mac Davis (1979)
- Barbara Mandrell & the Mandrell Sisters (1980)
- Mac Davis 10th Anniversary Special: I Still Believe in Music (1980)
- Lily: Sold Out (1981)
- Alvin and the Chipmunks (1983): voice only
- Today (1984-2017)
- Kenny & Dolly: A Christmas to Remember (1984)
- Kenny & Dolly: Real Love (1985)
- The Winning Hand (1985)
- Dolly (1987-1988)
- Bob Hope's Jolly Christmas Show (1988)
- Saturday Night Live (1989): also played various other roles
- Kenny, Dolly and Willie: Something Inside So Strong (1989)
- Designing Women (1990)
- Babes (1991)
- Big Dreams and Broken Hearts: The Dottie West Story (1995)
- Naomi & Wynonna: Love Can Build a Bridge (1995)
- Dolly Parton: Treasures (1996)
- Get to the Heart: The Barbara Mandrell Story (1997)

- The Simpsons (1999): voice only
- Jackie's Back (1999)
- Bette (2000)
- 17 Kids and Counting (2009)
- Dolly Celebrates 25 Years of Dollywood (2010)
- Strictly Come Dancing (2011)
- The Bachelorette (2012)
- A Country Christmas Story (2013)
- Kenny & Dolly: An Intimate Conversation (2013)
- Dolly Parton's Coat of Many Colors (2015): narrator
- Dolly Parton's Christmas of Many Colors: Circle of Love (2016): also played The Painted Lady
- Dolly & Friends: The Making of a Soundtrack (2018)
- Country Music (2019)
- Christmas at Dollywood (2019)
- CMT Giants: Kenny Rogers (2020)
- Biography: Dolly Parton (2020)
- Biography: Kenny Rogers (2020)
- A Holly Dolly Christmas (2020)

The following is a list of other television roles that Parton has played:

- A Smokey Mountain Christmas (1986): Lorna Davis
- Wild Texas Wind (1991): Thiola "Big T" Rayfield
- Heavens to Betsy (1994): Betsy Baxter
- Mindin' My Own Business (1994): Catering business owner
- Unlikely Angel (1996): Ruby Diamond
- The Magic School Bus (1996): Katrina Eloise "Murph" Murphy (voice)
- Blue Valley Songbird (1999): Leanna Taylor
- Reba (2005): Dolly Majors
- Hannah Montana (2006, 2007, 2010): Aunt Dolly
- Dolly Parton's Heartstrings (2019): various roles

The following is a list of Parton's film appearances:

- 9 to 5 (1980): Doralee Rhodes
- The Best Little Whorehouse in Texas (1982): Mona Stangley
- Rhinestone (194): Jake Farris
- Steel Magnolias (1989): Truvy Jones
- Straight Talk (1992): Shirlee Kenyon
- The Beverly Hillbillies (1993): herself
- Frank McKlusky, C.I. (2002): Edith McKlusky
- Miss Congeniality 2: Armed and Fabulous (2005): herself
- Gnomeo & Juliet (2011): Dolly Gnome (voice)
- The Year Dolly Parton Was My Mom (2011): herself (voice)
- Joyful Noise (2012): G.G. Sparrow
- Hollywood to Dollywood (2012): herself
- Dolly Parton's Christmas on the Square (2020): Angel

CHAPTER 12: AWARDS

The following is a list of awards granted to Parton by year:

1966
- BMI Awards Country Award

1968
- Cashbox Awards Most Promising Up and Coming Female Artist
- CMT Music Awards Duet of the Year and Most Promising Female Artist
- Country Music Association Awards Vocal Group of the Year
- Nashville Songwriters Association International Songwriter Achievement Award

1969
- CMT Music Awards Duet of the Year

1970
- CMT Music Awards Duet of the Year
- Country Music Association Awards Vocal Duo of the Year

1971
- Academy of Country Music Awards Top Vocal Group
- BMI Awards Country Award (2)
- CMT Music Awards TV Show of the Year
- Country Music Association Awards Vocal Duo of the Year
- Nashville Songwriters Association International Songwriter Achievement Award

1972
- BMI Awards Country Award
- Nashville Songwriters Association International Songwriter Achievement Award

1974
- BMI Awards Country Award (2) and Pop Award / Million-Air
- Nashville Songwriters Association International Songwriter Achievement Award

1975
- BMI Awards Country Award (4)
- Cashbox Awards Top Female Vocalist – Singles and Top Duo – Singles
- Country Music Association Awards Female Vocalist of the Year
- Nashville Songwriters Association International Songwriter Achievement Award (3)
- Record World Awards Tom Female Vocalist – Singles

1976
- BMI Awards Country Award (3)
- British Country Music Association Awards Female Vocalist of the Year

- Country Music Association Awards Female Vocalist of the Year
- Nashville Songwriters Association International Songwriter Achievement Award

1977

- BMI Awards Country Award
- British Country Music Association Awards Female Vocalist of the Year
- Cashbox Awards Female Entertainer of the Year – Country Albums, Female Vocalist of the Year – Country Albums, and Female Vocalist of the Year – Country Singles
- Record World Awards Top Female Vocalist – Albums

1978

- Academy of Country Music Awards Entertainer of the Year
- American Guild of Variety Artists Awards Country Star of the Year
- American Music Awards Favorite Country Album
- Billboard Country Artist of the Year, Country Singles Artist of the Year, and Bill Williams Memorial Artist of the Year
- BMI Awards Country Award (3) and Pop Award / Million-Air
- British Country Music Association Awards Female Vocalist of the Year
- Cashbox Awards Crossover Artist of the Year, Female Entertainer of the Year – Country Albums, Female Vocalist of the Year – Country Albums, and Female Vocalists – Highest Debut
- Country Music Association Awards Entertainer of the Year

1979

- American Guild of Variety Artists Awards Country Star of the Year

- BMI Awards Country Award (3) and Pop Award
- British Country Music Association Awards Female Vocalist of the Year
- Cashbox Awards Composer/Performer of the Year
- Grammy Awards Best Country Vocal Performance, Female
- Nashville Songwriters Association International Songwriter Achievement Award

1980
- American Guild of Variety Artists Awards Country Star of the Year and Entertainer of the Year
- British Country Music Association Awards Female Vocalist of the Year

1981
- Academy of Country Music Awards Top Female Vocalist
- Billboard Distinguished Achievement Award
- BMI Awards Country Award, Country Song of the Year, Pop Award / Million-Air, and Pop Song of the Year
- People's Choice Awards Favorite Song from a Motion Picture

1982
- BMI Awards Country Award (2) and Pop Award
- Grammy Awards Best Country Vocal Performance, Female and Best Country Song
- Nashville Songwriters Association International Songwriter Achievement Award

1983
- BMI Awards Country Award (3) and Pop Award

1984
- Academy of Country Music Awards Single Record of the Year – Artist and Top Vocal Duet
- American Music Awards Favorite Country Song

1985
- American Music Awards Favorite Country Song
- Canadian Country Music Association Top Selling Album of the Year
- Golden Raspberry Awards Worst Original Song

1986
- Ms. Magazine Woman of the Year

1988
- Academy of Country Music Awards Album of the Year – Artist
- CMT Music Awards Vocal Collaboration of the Year and Album of the Year
- Country Music Association Awards Vocal Event of the Year
- Grammy Awards Best Country Vocal Performance by a Duo or Group
- People's Choice Awards Favorite Female Performer in a New TV Program and Favorite All-Around Female Entertainer

1989
- Sevierville Chamber of Commerce Citizen of the Year

1990
- BMI Awards Country Award

1991
- Nashville Songwriters Association International Songwriter Achievement Award

1992
- CMT Music Awards Vocal Collaboration of the Year and Video of the Year
- Nashville Songwriters Association International Songwriter Achievement Award

1993

- BMI Awards Pop Award and Pop Song of the Year

1994
- BMI Awards Pop Award
- CMT Music Awards Living Legend Award, Minnie Pearl Humanitarian Award, and Vocal Event of the Year
- CMT Video Awards Video Event of the Year
- Soul Train Music Awards Song of the Year

1995
- BMI Awards Pop Award / Million-Air
- Nashville Songwriters Association International Songwriter Achievement Award

1996
- Country Music Association Awards Vocal Event of the Year

1999
- CMT Video Awards Video Event of the Year

2000
- Association for Independent Music Awards Best Bluegrass Album
- British Country Music Association Awards International Independent Artist
- CMT Music Awards Vocal Event of the Year
- Grammy Awards Best Country Vocal Collaboration
- International Bluegrass Music Awards Album of the Year

2001
- Grammy Awards Best Bluegrass Album

2002
- American Association of School Administrators Galaxy Award
- Association for Independent Music Awards Best Bluegrass Album
- Grammy Awards Best Female Country Vocal Perform-

- ance
- International Bluegrass Music Awards Recorded Event of the Year
- National State Teachers of the Year Chasing Rainbows Award

2003

- BMI Awards Icon Award
- Country Weekly Career Achievement Award
- Governor's Awards for the Arts Lifetime Achievement Award
- International Country Gospel Music Association Single of the Year
- Parents as Teachers National Center Child and Family Advocacy Award
- United States Fish and Wildlife Service Partnership Award

2004

- American Legion James V. Day Good Guy Award
- BBC Award
- Christian Fan Awards Duo of the Year and Song of the Year
- Library of Congress Living Legend Award
- International Bluegrass Music Awards Recorded Event of the Year
- NashvilleREAD Reading Works Award

2005

- Country Radio Broadcasters Career Achievement Award
- Sierra Awards Best Song
- United States Congress National Medal of Arts
- Academy of Country Music Awards Video of the Year – Artist and Vocal Event of the Year – Artist

2006

- CMT Music Awards Most Inspiring Video of the Year

- Country Music Association Awards Musical Event of the Year
- European Country Music Association Awards Vocal Collaboration of the Year
- Stennis Center for Public Service Lindy Boggs Award
- The Tennessean Tennessean of the Year

2007
- Academy of Country Music Awards Cliff Stone Pioneer Award
- Songwriters Hall of Fame Johnny Mercer Award
- Woodrow Wilson International Center for Scholars of the Smithsonian Institution Woodrow Wilson Public Service Award

2009
- Academy of Country Music Awards Jim Reeves International Award
- Broadway.com Audience Awards Favorite New Broadway Song
- Daughters of the American Revolution Founders Medal for Education
- Grand Master Fiddler Championship Dr. Perry F. Harris Award
- Los Angeles Drama Critics Circle Awards Best Musical Score
- Theatre Fans' Choice Awards Best Original Score
- TV Land Awards Most Memorable Female Guest Star in a Comedy as Herself

2011
- Grammy Lifetime Achievement Award

2012
- Nashville Songwriters Association International Song of the Year

2016

- Academy of Country Music Awards Tex Ritter Film Award
- Country Music Association Awards Willie Nelson Lifetime Achievement Award
- The Tennessean Tennessean of the Year

2017
- Academy of Country Music Awards Video of the Year – Artist and Gary Haber Lifting Lives Award
- Grammy Awards Best Country Duo/Group Performance
- International Bluegrass Music Awards Gospel Recorded Performance of the Year

2018
- Midsouth Emmy Awards Governors' Award for Lifetime Achievement and Outstanding Community Service Program

2019
- MusiCares Person of the Year

2020
- BMI Awards Million-Air (7)
- GLAAD Media Awards Best Individual Television Episode
- GMA Dove Award Short Form Video of the Year
- Grammy Awards Best Contemporary Christian Music Performance/Song

2021
- Grammy Awards Best Contemporary Christian Music Performance/Song
- K-Love Fan Awards Song of the Year
- Primetime Emmy Awards Outstanding Television Movie

Parton accepting the Woodrow Wilson Award

Manufactured by Amazon.ca
Bolton, ON